the ART
of WHY

Sandy,

Never stop pursuing

your WHY!

the ART of WHY

of WHY

By Frankie Russo

This book is dedicated to my wife Jess,
our three beautiful girls, Embry, Aria and Violet,
and everyone who is seeking to find their true
purpose and master it.

Table of
CONTENTS

THANK YOU

If there is one thing I have learned in the past 34 years, it's that I would never have been able to create something like this book or have any of the insights written, without help from my higher power whom I choose to call Jesus.

Jess is the love of my life and a big part of my WHY. Many times in the past 15 years, she has been the best of me. She showed me how important it was to stay passionate about my WHY even when I was very far from it. She has never stopped loving me and has allowed me the pleasure of walking in my true WHY: To be a Father.

My Parents and siblings were the first to believe in me. As early as I can remember, they never judged me for being an inventor and a little different. Even though most my experiments never worked, they still believed in me and encouraged me to always be myself.

Steve Pruett was the first person to ever show me what it looks like from 10,000 feet. He helped me see what was truly possible. This allowed me to believe in myself and that I didn't need to be afraid of failing.

Mignonne Wright saw something in me early on in my journey and was the one that ultimately helped me see not only that I could write this book but also why I should be writing it.

Dale Thevenet has helped me stay grounded over the past five years and showed me how to live one day at a time. He introduced me to a way of living that allows me the luxury of working my WHY (to help others) in a very real and consistent way.

My team at Potenza has played a vital role in helping my master my WHY, especially those who have been with me from the beginning like my brother Giorgio and Natalie Sandoz. Without them I would not have had the support I needed to do half of the things I've accomplished.

My early mentors like JD Pierce and Joey Russo taught me so much about the basics of how to run a business. They also helped ingrain the necessity of a strong work ethic that would help me get to the finish line

LEARNING
from the Masters

"The two most important days in your life are the day you are born and the day you find out **WHY**."

— Mark Twain

Walt Disney wanted to spark creativity and awaken the child in every person on the planet. Fred Smith wanted to get a package from point A to point B, and he wanted to do it faster than anybody else. Coco Chanel wanted to revolutionize the fashion industry.

What did these three pioneers have in common? Each one knew **WHY** they did what they did.

Here is what I know for sure. You were born for a purpose! You were born to forge a unique path! How do I know this? You are reading this book. You are seeking higher ground, better answers, another way. You may have noticed that the world is full of sheep – flocks of people following the pack. They are walking a path with no idea why or where they want to end up. I know this because I used to be one of those sheep. I was following the purpose of others instead of my own. And my motives were shallow and self-centered.

Washington Irving said, "Great minds have purpose; others have wishes." Asking yourself why you are here gives your journey purpose. It takes the wishes you have for your life and gives them meaning.

Of course, people may have vague descriptions of where they want to end up. There are some who say "I want to be happy" or "I want to be successful" or "I want to be healthy." But few people stop to ask WHY. And even fewer stick with the question long enough to find out the answer. Those who do create Mickey Mouse, overnight shipping companies, and Chanel Number 5.

I've spent years of soul searching to discover and then master the art of my **WHY**. I have realized my **WHY** is helping other people get what they need. It's the the most fulfilling act I can do. Ultimately, it's why I'm here. That's the reason I turned my **WHY** into an art form I was determined to master.

Although I have tried many ways to perfect my purpose I found the steps in this book never fail me. I can apply them to any aspect of my life or any goal I set out to achieve. In this book I am applying them to my ultimate **WHY,** my reason for living. But feel free to apply them elsewhere as well.

There are ten steps to mastering your **WHY**. The first five are the "Start-Up Steps." Working them reminds me of the way bamboo grows. For the first four years it's a puny little tree and there is little outward growth. But in the fifth year bamboo can easily grow 80 feet. These first five steps are like the beginning of the bamboo tree and will be the foundation for your success. Take your time with each step. If you find yourself struggling it's OK to go back if you need to rework a previous one. But you must work the first five before moving to the second half of the master plan!

Steps 6-10 are the "Lifestyle Steps." And they are a bit different. The principles of these steps can be worked daily. They may take you longer to work through completely. They might not come in order. And you should not rush the process as you are working towards mastering your **WHY**. It's important to realize the Lifestyle Steps need to be worked in a way that is realistic for you! There is no perfect way to work them. So adapt them for your lifestyle and be gentle with yourself through the process.

There have been countless times where these steps have profoundly changed many lives. If you work these steps you will find yourself a different person from the one you are today.

It's important to remember that perfecting any art form takes daily practice and dedication. Think of all the greats in cinema, music, art, and sports. Think of the time and dedication each took to be the best. Being considered one of the best doesn't happen overnight.

It took Michael Jordan seven seasons to win a world championship. Imagine the countless hours of practice he had under his belt before he ever got to hold that first trophy? How many years of research do you think a scientist commits to find a cure? Many artist spend years working on a single art piece. Just think of Michelangelo. Painting the ceiling of the Sistine Chapel took years!

I want you to begin thinking of your life as an art form that needs to be mastered. All artists have tools or a medium they use for their craft. Consider your purpose to be your medium.

Malcolm Gladwell said in his book *Outliers* that it can take 10,000 hours for an artist to master their art form. How many hours have you spent perfecting yours? How much time have you invested in answering the question "**WHY** am I doing what I'm doing?"

As you walk your path, understand you'll have a lot of work to do. This journey requires complete honesty and humility. You cannot master your **WHY** unless you are first honest about where you are right now.

Remember you will get what you put into this process so invest in yourself. You are worth it! Use this book to understand what it will take to be the best version of you so you may live with purpose.

Take a few seconds to gather some supplies. Grab a notebook or a journal, a couple of pens, and a highlighter. Each chapter has an exercise for you to complete. Feel free to mark up the book or write in the margin at the bottom of each page.

A good friend of mine gave me a copy of the poem *Desiderata*. I've included the text below. Written by Max Ehrman, it's one of the greatest poems I have ever read in relation to living life right. The only thing I would add to the end of the poem is "Find your purpose and then work one day at a time to master it."

Desiderata

Go placidly amid the noise and haste, and remember what peace there may be in silence.

As far as possible, without surrender, be on good terms with all persons.

Speak your truth quietly and clearly; and listen to others, even the dull and ignorant; they too have their story.

Avoid loud and aggressive persons; they are vexatious to the spirit.

If you compare yourself with others, you may become vain and bitter, for always there will be greater and lesser persons than yourself.

Enjoy your achievements as well as your plans.

Keep interested in your own career, however humble; it is a real possession in the changing fortunes of time.

Exercise caution in your business affairs; for the world is full of trickery.

But let this not blind you to what virtue there is; many persons strive for high ideals, and everywhere life is full of heroism.

Be yourself.

Especially do not feign affection.

Neither be cynical about love; for in the face of all aridity and disenchantment, it is as perennial as the grass.

Take kindly the counsel of the years, gracefully surrendering the things of youth.

Nurture strength of spirit to shield you in sudden misfortune. But do not distress yourself with dark imaginings.

Many fears are born of fatigue and loneliness. Beyond a wholesome discipline, be gentle with yourself.

You are a child of the universe no less than the trees and the stars; you have a right to be here.

And whether or not it is clear to you, no doubt the universe is unfolding as it should.

Therefore be at peace with God, whatever you conceive Him to be. And whatever your labors and aspirations, in the noisy confusion of life, keep peace with your soul.

With all its sham, drudgery and broken dreams, it is still a beautiful world. Be cheerful. Strive to be happy.

My wish is that you use this book as a manual and a road map to help you master your own **WHY**. By working these steps you'll discover new pathways to success that once remained hidden. You'll begin to look at life's challenges with a much healthier perspective. You'll start turning your challenges into opportunities. And you'll begin to form relationships that are mutually rewarding.

I hope my story—the good, the great, and the ugly—shed a light of hope and clarity on the path to mastering your **WHY**.

Now let's get started!

STEP 1
Know Your Why

"I believe a purpose is something for which one is responsible; it's not just divinely assigned."

— Michael J. Fox

I remember every single detail about the day I hit rock bottom. The house was empty—the kind of vacant that scares a grown man. And that day, it seemed there was an actual sound to silence. All I could hear was the creak of the floor and the dust rearranging itself when the heater kicked on. There was no doubt I was all alone, and I could not for the life of me understand why.

I had been on top of the world—making more money than I could spend. I was living fast and free, and enjoying every single minute of it. And it was so easy. I had found a way to compartmentalize every part of my life. I was a loving husband. I was a brilliant businessman and a great boss. I had no shortage of friends, and life was good. Or so I thought.

So what had gone wrong? What was I doing alone, broke, and afraid? It turns out the truth really does hurt. Especially when I had to admit I was actually a terrible husband and a lousy businessman. And realizing that the only friends I had were simply there to share my drugs and feed the lies I was telling myself.

That day, alone in the house, was when I was at my lowest point —the end of myself. It took my wife leaving me to realize just how lost I was. And for all my efforts to be powerful, great, and important, I had nothing to show for it.

They say the darkest hour is before dawn. I believe the darkest time is before you find out **WHY** you are here. It took a cold, hard slap of reality for me to finally realize I needed a better way of life.

I had to admit, I wasn't where I wanted to be. I found myself wondering, ***WHY** am I here?* I longed to truly understand *my purpose for living*. This book is my story of how, once I discovered my WHY, I went on to master it. Now it's time for you to do the same!

Welcome to Step One, where you start with your WHY. This step is the foundation for the entire process of mastering the art of your **WHY**. Taking some time to unlock the answers that will show you your "WHY" is imperative. And it's not negotiable.

When I was young, I thought I would grow up to be a mad scientist! I was at home in my lab while everyone else was outside playing. I would be working on a moon rocket, time machine, jet pack, glider, lasers, and even a hoverboard. No matter what idea I had I never had any doubt about my inventions capacity for successful operation.

My **WHY** as a child was to create something grand that would improve the world around me. But as time went by and I got older, having a purpose just didn't seem important to me. It wasn't something I even thought much about. So life happened.

Because I wasn't aware of my **WHY**, I let the world make decisions for me. I was fixated on fame and fortune. All I wanted was more money, more notoriety, and more people around me telling me I was important.

But **why** did I yearn for these things? I wanted them because I needed to feel like I mattered. And so I put myself first in every aspect of my life. I neglected the people who loved me the most because I was completely self-absorbed and lost.

For a long time I blamed sex, drugs, and rock and roll as the reason for losing my way. They were only a symptom of the real problem. The real issue was ME.

Once I looked in the mirror, I had to get honest with myself. This honesty and truth about where I had gone off the rails was the beginning of my road to freedom. It was the first time I understood the concept of living with a purpose.

When I reached rock bottom I was forced to really dig deep and ask myself, *what the hell am I doing with my life?* I had come to the end of the road, and I had no direction for where to go next. I had to admit I was lost.

Finding my WHY started with being honest that my life had become out of control. Losing my wife, business, and reputation were evidence of this. If the problem was me, then I knew that without enlisting the help of others, I would not be able to fix it. I started taking direction from other people who had climbed out of the pits. I sought out people who discovered their own paths to happiness and freedom.

Being accountable to others was a huge shift for me and it was not easy. Before hitting bottom, I thought I only answered to God and The IRS, and even those I didn't fear too much. I was running my own life and it was a train wreck. Getting real about the fact that I couldn't do it alone was a major step for me. In fact, building a team is so important I have an entire chapter dedicated to this in step 4.

By asking "**WHY** am I here?" I discovered my true purpose in life is to focus on helping others. I began the journey of discovering my true motives, which in time would define my life's purpose. One day at a time, my course and my direction started to change.

Which leads me to why I called this book the "Art of Why." Art is never perfect and never finished. The Art of WHY is about the journey, not some trophy or guru status. Each person is the master of their own life; the artist in their story. This book is a handful of my experiences and is by no means gospel. I wrote this in the hopes to help people master their why and see that their life is an art form.

And now comes THE MOST IMPORTANT STEP in this entire process; TAKING ACTION! That's right! It's time for you to take action. You will be given lots of great information throughout this book. That information will only become useful when you actually USE it! This is the beginning of your exciting new journey. By taking the actions recommended in this book, today could become the first day of the best of your life. Are you READY? Let's dive in!

The Art of Why

STEP 1
EXERCISE

Contemplate

Devote some time to quiet contemplation. You'll want to think about where you are and exactly where it is you'd like to be. Consider the path before you and imagine what the journey is going to be like. You need to devote time to pondering the questions in the exercises. Be still and listen to your thoughts.

Formulate

Write the following questions:

"Where am I right now on this journey of life? Am I at my bottom? Am I enjoying the view from the top of the world? Or am I somewhere between?"

    1. "Why am I here [in this spot]?"

        ....

        ....

        ....

2. "Why am I here [on earth]?"

....

....

....

3. "Am I fulfilled?"

....

....

....

4. "Am I helping others find fulfillment?"

....

....

....

Take time to listen to the answers as they enter your thoughts. Write down what you are thinking.

Activate

Review your answers to the above questions and write out what you believe your purpose is. Make a list of all the benefits of what your life will be like as you start to really live out your WHY.

....

....

....

....

....

....

STEP 2
Make a Plan

"There are some people who live in a dream world, and there are some who face reality; and then there are those who turn one into the other."

— **Douglas H. Everett**

Imagine traveling from New York to Los Angeles. You have no mode of transportation, no maps, and no GPS. You just know the general direction you need to travel is west. So you set out on foot to begin the journey. How long would it take you to walk to California? Would you make it? What obstacles would you face? Would you give up along the way?

It would be foolish to attempt the journey without the appropriate tools and a plan. Realistically, it would take months to walk the distance. Odds are you probably wouldn't make it.

When we want to travel from Point A to Point B, we map out the journey ahead of time. We book a flight. We make reservations at a hotel. We plan for the weather by checking what the temperature will be on the dates we are in town.

If we travel by car, we use GPS to give us turn-by-turn directions or we have a map to follow. We pack basic necessities like toiletries, clothes, shoes, and an umbrella in case of rain. We check out restaurants in the area for where we may want to eat. We buy tickets for shows or museums we might want to visit. Some people plan every detail of a trip. How crazy is it that we invest this much time in planning a one-week vacation but we don't take any time to plan our lives?

I've learned the hard way that operating without a plan is like walking from New York to Los Angeles without a map. It can be challenging to plan if you are a spontaneous person like me. If you ask my wife or any of my friends, they'll tell you I'm impulsive. I have a hundred ideas a day and I'm always ready to get started. But I've learned the ones who succeed are the ones who plan things out.

So what will you need to succeed? How much time will it take? What are the steps to mastering your WHY? What tools are essential? What realities will you have to face? What hardships might you need to overcome? Benjamin Franklin said it best: "If you fail to plan, you are planning to fail." That's why you must invest in Step 2. To succeed in tackling this step, you will have to take time to *Make a Plan*.

Most companies begin with some type of a business plan. Having one makes you stop long enough to research decisions before diving in blindly. The process forces you to consider things like cash flow and how many staff members you will need. This process will ask you to compare your business to your competitors.

When I started a mortgage company, I didn't make a business plan. My only plan was to sell **more**. This model actually worked for a couple of years. But I didn't know at the time there was a national mortgage crisis around the corner. I didn't look to the historical data and plan for the inevitable rainy days. I just assumed our company would always be on a roll and flush with money.

When the mortgage crisis and recession hit in 2008, I wasn't ready. I had to sell my car in order to keep my office open. I walked to work for over a year. This is the kind of thing that happens when you fail to plan.

That year was a major turning point for me both professionally and personally. Those hard times forced me to get serious about why I was in business in the first place. I made some challenging decisions. I closed down one company and focused on a new one, Potenza. That was the first time my business plan focused 100% on helping people and building our name. Money was no longer my purpose. It was now just a by-product of a grander vision. I knew I had to become a servant leader and make everything about others. Without a plan I wouldn't be where I am today.

Let's talk about your plan. And we'll use health as an example. If you have a goal to live a healthy life, then you need to get real about what it will take to make that happen! You need to create your plan of action; otherwise that goal is nothing more than a wish. Will you join a gym or invest in equipment for your home? Will you work out alone or with a trainer? Will you exercise once a week or four times a week? Will you change your eating habits or will you only exercise? The bottom line is you have to consider what works for you, your life, and your schedule. You have to be realistic. *And you have to male a plan.*

I have a friend who has tried every diet out there. By his own admission his failure is based on wanting quick results. He hasn't focused on the long term planning. He never determined what is required to lose weight and maintain a healthy lifestyle. He never sought the advice of a doctor. He just wanted to lose weight and it wanted to do it fast! If he had taken the time to plan for the life changes and sacrifices he may have reached his goal.

But, I have a friend who planned everything. She counted the cost up front. She knew it would take some time to change her relationship with food. She understood her limitations and knew she could not make drastic changes or she would fail in the long run. She took it one step at a time and started walking just a little each day. She took baby steps.

After several months of walking, she picked up the pace. She *slowly* changed her eating habits. After about a year, she started running. It took her an entire year to start running! Because she planned for it, she succeeded and lost over 100 pounds.

So are you ready to make a plan? Let's map out your path to the rewards you are seeking. As you work this step, I invite you to stop and consider what it will *really* take to master the art of your WHY. What will you need to invest? What sacrifices will you need to make? What obstacles might you encounter and how can you stay on track when you do?

Success worth having is success worth planning. Counting the cost on the front end will bring you one step closer to mastering the Art of your WHY.

STEP 2
EXERCISE

Formulate

Review your notes from the "EXERCISE" section of the previous step. Consider where it is you would like to go. What is your ultimate destination? Write it down and then answer the following questions.

What steps will I need to take to reach my desired destination?

1. When do I start?

   ....

   ....

2. Whom can I speak to for guidance? Who has been where I want to go and can show me the way?

   ....

   ....

3. Where can I find resources that will assist me on this journey?

....

....

It's important that you WRITE out your answers and don't just leave them as thoughts. I write down my goals as part of committing to the process. I found early on in business if my goals are not written down, I usually don't complete them.

And there is science to back it up. Dr. Gail Matthews proved in a study you are 42% more likely to achieve your goals by simply writing them down.

Plus, something magical happens when your dream goes from your head to a piece of paper. It makes the goal real and obtainable. Writing your goals down helps you clarify what you want. It motivates you to take action and helps you track your progress.

Formulate

What will mastering your WHY cost?

....

How much time will I need to devote?

....

How much money will this require?

....

Will the rewards be greater than the investment?

....

Activate

Schedule your next steps.

Put the time on your calendar.

Make the appropriate appointments.

Stay focused on the path to your dreams!

STEP 3
Commit and Believe

"I am the greatest.
I said that even before I knew I was."

— Muhammad Ali

At this point the voice inside your head may start to question your ability to make your WHY a reality. Loved ones may also voice concern over whether you are going down the right path. It might seem at every turn there is someone lurking to plant a seed of doubt in your mind. Imagine there is a gatekeeper at the door and refuse entry! YOU CAN DO THIS!

Henry Ford once said, "Whether you think you can, or you think you can't—you're right." This step is about committing to go all the way and making a decision to believe in your journey.

One of the greatest examples of commitment comes from one of the greatest losers of all time. John Stephan Akwhari was a marathon runner from Tanzania. Akwhari represented his country in the 1968 Olympics. He had dreams of feeling a medal being placed around his neck. But after the race started, it wasn't long before he lagged behind.

After 18.5 miles he collapsed. He was struggling to breathe, his legs were injured, and the Olympic officials urged him to quit. He refused. Over an hour after the winner was announced and all the others had finished the race he was still running. Most of the spectators had gone home when Akwhari made it across the finish line and collapsed. When a reporter asked him later why he continued to run, he said, "My country did not send me to start the race. They sent me to finish."

Akwhari ran in the Olympics to honor his country, and nothing was going to stop him from finishing that race. His commitment to the goal far outweighed the pain and struggle he endured to make his dream a reality.

Akwhari was committed to his WHY. He knew that by paying attention to the time or even the other runners, he might get discouraged. His WHY was to honor his country by crossing the finish line. He committed to it, he believed in his ability to make it happen and he never wavered. Akwhari exemplified the true definition of commitment.

Why is the step so important? Because, like Akwhari, you will undoubtedly face obstacles. You will most likely endure struggles and maybe even pain as you work to bring your own dreams to reality.

Many things will conspire to prevent you from even seeing the finish line. Don't let interruptions in your schedule, stress, and doubt keep you from crossing it.

So commit to your dream and believe you will achieve it. Start by changing the way you think and speak. Your thoughts turn into your words. Your words turn into your actions. Your actions develop into habits and your habits form your character. So start by refusing to engage in negative thoughts. Change the way you think and speak so your actions will naturally follow. The power of positive thinking is undeniable. You get more of what you focus on. Mother Theresa once said she would never go to an anti-war rally. But if she were invited to a peace rally she would be there! She understood the difference in the language used for two incredibly similar events! One was negative and one was positive although they both served the same purpose.

Change your words and you will change your results! Use words that empower, uplift and encourage you to continue going for the gold! Don't say "If". Say "When." "If" tells your subconscious mind that the probability is unlikely. Saying "when" to your subconscious mind removes all doubt.

Napoleon Hill was one of the pioneers in the self-help industry. He developed the 17 Principles of the Science of Success. He wrote several books, including *Law of Success* and *Think and Grow Rich*. Hill once said, "You can be anything you want to be, if only you believe with sufficient conviction and act in accordance with your faith; for whatever the mind can conceive and believe, the mind can achieve."

To help you believe you can take a note from Noah St. John, founder of Power Habits Academy. He wrote an article in The Huffington Post saying that everyone needs to find a loving mirror. This is a person who believes in you, he says, when you don't believe in yourself. When you are full of self-doubt, this is the one you turn to. He or she is your support. For me, it's my wife, Jess. But it can be a friend, family member, or coworker.

Another tool to help you solidify your belief is to envision it as if it has already happened. Imagine you are working your dream job. How would you dress? How would you feel? How would you behave? Hold the vision and start living that way now. Don't wait.

Lean on the understanding that you are enough and remember why you are on this path. Use positive affirmations. Envision the goal as if it's already happened, believe in your abilities and GO FOR IT!

It's time to commit and believe.

The Art of Why

STEP 3
EXERCISE

Contemplate

Review the "exercises" from the previous steps so that they are fresh in your mind. Remember to use positive language in your thinking and speaking. This will lead to positive actions.

Think of a power statement you can use every day that will keep you motivated to move forward. It might be something like, "I am enough. I have within me and within my reach, everything I need to [insert WHY.] For example cross that finish line and honor my country; earn the gold medal; positively impact 1 million lives with my widget, etc.}

Formulate

Watch your everyday language for verbal roadblocks. Make a list of common negative phrases you use. Write new phrases that focus on the solution or a positive spin on the topic.

Here are a few examples:

Don't say, "Constructive criticism. Say, **"Feedback."**

Don't say, "No problem." Say, **"Definitely!"**

Don't say, "Can't complain." Say, **"Everything is going well, thanks!"**

Don't say, "I'm exhausted." Say, **"I need a vacation."**

Don't say, "There is no way I can do this." Say, **"How can I be successful?"**

Activate

Review your power statement every day to strengthen your belief and commitment. Create a contract with yourself. Make a commitment, in writing, to master your WHY. Use the steps you detailed before and include them in your contract. Sign it. You can find a sample contracts on our **website at theartofwhy. com**. Be sure to have a witness (perhaps your loving mirror) sign the contract as well. Put you plan into action by committing to the road ahead!

STEP 4
Build Your Team

"Coming together is a beginning.
Keeping together is progress.
Working together is success."

—Henry Ford

The goal in a football game is to get the ball into your opponents' end zone more than they get it in yours. That's it.

It doesn't seem all that complicated.

So how many positions are on an American football team? First, you have the offense. That includes the center, guards, offensive tackles, tight ends, wide receivers, fullback, running back, tailback, H-back, wingback, slotback and quarterback.

Then, you have the defensive team. Which includes the defensive end, defensive tackle, linebacker, cornerback, safety, nickelbacks, and dimebacks.

And let's not forget about the special teams' positions. Let's see, there's the kicker, holder, long snapper, kick returner, punter, punt returner, gunner, and wedge buster.

All these people work together towards one goal.

They move a small sphere covered in pigskin 100 yards down a grass-covered field.

Every position plays a part in the team's success. Now, imagine you are the quarterback. You can't walk out on the field alone and expect to win against another team. It just won't happen.

Think about every awards show you ever watched. The acceptance speeches are based on thanking a team of people who are responsible for the win.

Step 4 is "***Build Your Team***". It's crucial to your success for you to accept the fact that you can't do it alone. You are going to need the support of other people. Step 4 is also about relying on something greater than yourself to master your WHY.

For me, that something starts with my faith. Most of us have heard that nothing is impossible with God on our side. It's amazing how much your faith grows when you actually witness an act of God firsthand.

My first memory of seeing God's great work happened when I was 6 years old. My family left everything in Louisiana and moved to Pittsburgh. My parents became inner-city missionaries to the homeless.

As you can imagine, this change came with many

financial hardships. During one particularly tough time, the last of our food money ran out and we had nothing to eat. I sat in the kitchen that night with my father, mother, and two brothers. We had no idea where we would get food that evening, so we prayed as a family that God would somehow supply dinner. The hours wore on and our bellies began to growl. At that moment someone who knew we were missionaries showed up at our door unsolicited. They brought food for our entire family.

That night, my life changed. That one simple meal shaped my beliefs in a way that still holds true today. Some might write this off as sheer coincidence. But I know better. There have been hundreds of different God experiences that have truly strengthened my faith. The more I trust and believe, the easier it is to step out into the darkness; where so many are too afraid to ever venture.

As a child, I believed a higher power played a necessary role in my life. But as an adult, I had lost confidence in that higher power. I became more and more independent.

As I grew older, my theory changed. When it came to work I believed if you wanted something done right, you needed to do it yourself. It was my go-to for everything I accomplished. I could do it smarter, better, and faster. Relying on anyone else was just a fool's game.

Because things in my marriage and my business seemed to be going well, I was happy to take credit for it all. I was drawn deeper and deeper into what I like to call my "how great thou art" phase. Alcohol and drugs were my religion of choice, and I turned my back on God and my wife.

For a while, my do-it-yourself philosophy seemed to work. My happy hour started with cocktails then quickly morphed into drugs. I rationalized my behavior as "just doing business." And I even made myself believe it for a while.

But as I relied more on myself and less on my support team, everything started to fall apart.

I got caught using drugs and I lost everything including my wife. I crashed hard. I realized I had only one option. I needed to get sober. And I had to start by admitting I couldn't do it alone.

My only option was to go back to relying on something greater than myself. That was the first time in years I turned to God. That was more than eight years ago, and I've been sober ever since. By taking the steps in this book, my wife came back to me and our family has never been stronger. In fact, we are expecting our third child!

I have experienced countless blessings over the past few years. These were a direct result of making the decision to trust in God. And I've been inspired by the twelve-step program that I follow to focus on others instead of myself. I have a group of friends who bring out the best in me. And at my company, I'm honored to work alongside some of the greatest minds in my industry. I've surrounded myself with truly great team members.

At this stage of the game, I had determined my WHY and I had made a plan. I committed to that plan and I believed that I could see it through to completion. I turned to God and followed where he was leading me. I began to add strong accountability partners and "love mirrors" to my team. I started putting in the work. And before I knew it, I turned around to see new evidence of God's goodness and the strength He gave me. This practice of faith is a cornerstone for mastering my WHY.

I realize now the importance of trusting in God. It has never been more evident to me that I can't do it alone. I know how to take individuals and form a team that is stronger together than they ever were apart. I see, as the saying goes, that "teamwork makes the dream work."

Even after I created my team I still felt like there was still something missing. I needed a coach. I needed someone who had already walked the path of success. I needed an individual who could share the in's and out's of life based on the journey they had mastered.

I'll never forget the day Steve Pruett offered to mentor me. He is a brilliant and successful businessman and I was excited to meet with him. We sat down for lunch and there was a unique connection in that first meeting. Before even finishing our meal, Steve was offering to help my business in any way he could. It was the beginning of what would be an important relationship on my journey to mastering my WHY.

Over the years, Steve and I have become like family. I've learned so much from having someone who understands what success looks like. He holds me accountable. But he does it while sharing with me his vision for my future. He has seen a picture much larger than what I could ever have envisioned for myself. Sometimes you need to borrow other people's belief until you have enough of your own.

As you build your own team, I encourage you to

look for someone like Steve. You need someone who can teach you to stay cool, calm, and collected in the heat of the battle. You need someone to lean on during those times when nothing seems to be going right.

One of my most beloved mentors is my wife Jess. Not only does she just get me, Jess also grounds me. I know she wants what is best for our family and me. I also know that she loves me enough to always be honest and not just tell me what I want to hear. I must always stay humble and be willing to take direction for my mentors to really be able to help me.

Besides Steve and Jess I have my twelve step sponsor Dale. Our relationship is also vital in helping me keep my WHY in perspective on a daily basis. He is another person in my life who will call me out when I get off track. I can't get anything by him. I rarely make decisions without talking to him first. I've learned to take direction from someone else. He doesn't always agree with me. And that's OK. But I've learned to strongly consider his advice and think it through. Taking direction from someone else and has served me well in so many scenarios over the years. Our relationship has taught me the true value of being humble.

Having mentors who can speak honestly in your life will allow you to see the many angles of any problem. Then you can turn those challenges into opportunities.

If you are a dreamer, like me, you will need someone to keep you grounded. This person will bring you back down from the clouds and help you look at things more realistically. If there are any holes in your big ambitions, this person will help you find them. You can analyze numbers, look at statistics, and get along just fine.

Your next team member may be your cheerleader. They will believe in you every step of the way. They will push you to do more because they believe you could move Mt. Everest on your own. They are warm to every idea you have and will support you no matter what the idea may be!

So who is going to help you move the mountain? Who is going to be there when you need timely advice?

When you do find a mentor, be sure to define what you are expecting from them. You need to know what position they will play for you. And most importantly, make sure the mentor you choose has something you want.

STEP 4

EXERCISE

Contemplate

Review the exercises from the previous steps so they are fresh in your mind. Consider your relationship with a higher power than yourself. Do you have faith? Do you trust in God? Do you know that God wants even greater things for you than you can even think or imagine?

Formulate:

Answer the following questions:

1. Who GETS me? Who is in my corner? Who wants the best for me?

   ....

   ....

   ....

2. Who will lift me up AND ALSO tell it like it is? Who loves enough to be honest while also being supportive of my dreams?

....

....

....

3. Who has "been there done that?" If I could choose my own dream mentor, whom might that be?

....

....

....

4. Who else do I need to add to my team? What positions can I hire out or delegate so that I can maximize my time and operate only in the areas in which I excel?

....

....

....

Activate:

Find a mentor or hire a coach.

Get an accountability partner.

Hire team members in the areas that are not your strength. Or recruit people to help you with your day-to-day life so you can spend time operating in your best zone.

STEP 5
START

"You don't have to be great to start.
But you have to start to be great."

— Zig Ziglar

Thomas Jefferson Snodgrass, Sergeant Fathom, and W. Epaminondas Adrastus Blab all had one thing in common. They would not have existed if it weren't for someone just starting.

A young steamboat captain dreamed up each of these fictitious writers. It was his way of getting his writing into people's hands without having to put his real name on it. Fortunately for the literary world, the young Samuel Clemens decided to *start*. And because he did, he found a way to dip his foot into the waters of writing and publishing. And through this journey, another name was born: Mark Twain!

The young writer said, "The secret to getting ahead is getting started."

This principle is Step 5 in a nutshell. It is where the real work begins. It has taken preparation to get to this point. You have been focusing on determining your **WHY** and making a plan of action. You've made a commitment to see the plan through to fruition. Then backed it up with a strong belief in making the dream a reality. You've built a strong team to assist you in reaching your ultimate destination. The prep work is complete. Now, it's time to get down to business and take action.

People who succeed do so because they start putting one foot in front of the other. Now is the time to put your WHY into practice!

I'll never forget the day I became willing to put in the hard work it takes to succeed. I had been working an outside sales job as an account executive in advertising. My mindset at the time was to do as little as possible to make enough money to live.

Since I was the breadwinner in the family I thought it was okay to play video games with my younger brother and his friends during my free time. One day, my wife got fed up with me complaining about how I didn't have any clients. She called me out on all the excuses I gave her and at that moment I decided to go to work. I closed two new prospects by 5 p.m. Ever since that day, I've committed to never looking back. I'm still amazed how much I can do when I start.

I read an article a few years ago based on a study

of gifted children. The study followed these kids throughout their lives. The researchers found those who worked harder lived longer than the happy-go-lucky-do-just-enough-to-get-by people. The ones who took on more responsibility were more likely to live longer and healthier lives.

The saying "Idle hands are the devil's playground" is ancient. But the idea is still relative today.

The longer you wait to start, the more likely you are to give up before you even begin. Most people will never achieve greatness because they lack the willingness to get started. They will make lists, research, and even ask for opinions. Many people spend their entire lives in the preparation mode. They are so busy *preparing* to start they never actually DO IT.

Getting started is often the toughest part of one's weight loss journey. The fitness and health club industry makes an incredible amount of money because of this fact. Let's take a look. One national health club chain has an average of 6,500 members at each location on the books at any given time. Yet, their facilities can only serve an average of 300 members.

How can this business model work? Because people have the best intentions. They buy the right clothes, sign up for a membership and schedule their workouts. They find exercises they would like to use in a routine they plan to do once they get to the gym. But the majority of those who sign up never show up…in other words, they never start. And most gyms wouldn't survive if they did.

This doesn't just happen with fitness. I am shocked at the lengths some people will go to prevent getting down to business. They procrastinate and make excuses. The actual work becomes harder for them because they just don't start the process.

The task may seem too big at first glance, which is one reason the prep work IS so important. You need to do the first four steps. But then it is crucial that you jump right in and start the second you've finished steps 1 through 4.

One of the best examples of someone who encompasses the first four steps of this book is Nolan Bushnell. You are probably thinking, *who the heck is he?* While you may not know his name, I'm sure you know his products.

Nolan is an entrepreneur, technology pioneer, and scientist. The man, who has been called the father of video game industry, is the founder of both Atari and Chuck E. Cheese. He's helped big name businesses like IBM and Cisco Systems.

Taking quick action could easily be Nolan's mantra. One thing about Nolan is that he is not afraid to start. He said, "The critical ingredient is getting off your butt and doing something. It's as simple as that. A lot of people have ideas, but there are few who decide to do something about them now. Not tomorrow. Not next week. But today."

So what drives Nolan? He's passionate. He doesn't flinch when it comes to starting processes he believes in. He is driven by "enhancing and improving the educational process..." He has a higher purpose, and he knows his WHY.

What does this step look like? It's not the day your register to go back to school. It's the moment you actually enter that classroom on day one. It's when you step onto that treadmill or show up for the yoga class. You take a sledgehammer to the wall in your house where you want to build the new addition. You record a demo track. You write the first line of code or apply for a patent. Whatever your passion—your WHY—now is the time to take the first step to make it a reality.

The philosopher, Arthur Schopenhauer, once said, "Ordinary people think merely of spending time; great people think of using it." Now is the time to get up and get going! It's time to stop spending your time and start using it!

Speaking of time, here's an interesting fact that might motivate you. The World Health Organization has estimated the life span of an American to be 41,942,880 seconds long. Sounds like a lot! But believe me, they'll disappear faster than you may think. If you have reached the age of 25, you have already lived almost 16 million of those seconds. Make each one count, and start on the road to success today! Whatever your excuse is, don't flinch and just start!

STEP 5
EXERCISE

Contemplate:

Review the exercises from the previous steps so they're fresh in your mind. Take your plan of action and chunk it down into baby steps so it will seem easier to actually start.

Formulate:

Write down your answer to these questions:

1. What is one baby step I can take TODAY to move me closer to my ultimate goal?

    ....

    ....

    ....

2. By taking this baby step, will I be closer to mastering the art of my WHY?

    ....

    ....

    ....

Activate

START!!!

Complete the baby step from above. Then determine what the next baby step will be and do that. Each day, take at least one baby step towards your goal. Consistency will lead you to your destination.

STEP 6
Be Patient and Persistent

"Patience, persistence and perspiration make an unbeatable combination for success."

— **Napoleon Hill**

At this point the ball is rolling and you have really started working on mastering your purpose. There is nothing sweeter than that first taste of success. All those ideas, dreams and dogged determination are starting to pay off. You are halfway there!

Step 6 is the beginning of the "Lifestyle Steps." The results of the next five steps will differ for everyone. And the pace you work through them will vary as well. Don't rush. Understand that each of these steps is an important part of your journey or a phase you must go through. And the second half of mastering your WHY is where the real skills are developed.

The foundation for Step 6 is this: nothing in life comes easily. Those who win over the long run are those with patience. It's the ones who dig in deep and are willing to invest back in themselves and their journey. They keep moving forward even when they feel like giving up.

It's important to start with patience. We've all heard patience is a virtue. Patience is a virtue. But not an easy one! In fact for Sir James Dyson it sucked, literally. James first had the idea for his revolutionary vacuum cleaner when he was in his 30's. The story is simple enough, he owned a Hoover and it lost suction. It's been said necessity is the mother of invention. To clean his floors James needed his vacuum to suck.

He rolled up his sleeves, mustered a ton of patience, and tried over and over to create his invention. He tried 5,126 times before he finally succeeded at the age of 36.

The disposable vacuum bag industry was worth over $140 million at the time. Companies weren't eager to embrace his new idea of developing a bagless device. He was unable to find a distributor in his country. James could not be deterred. He went to Japan and released a hot pink vacuum cleaner that went on to win Japanese design awards. Even then it was three years before he received his first patent. Still, he could not find a distributor. So he started his own company. Ten years after he first succeeded he was finally able to distribute it himself.

The definition of patience isn't waiting. It's waiting

without complaint in situations that could cause discomfort. The fact Dyson wasn't an inventor and knew nothing about the vacuum industry didn't stop him. He was patient as he researched and learned the best way to bring his idea to life. I imagine it was frustrating to have over 5,000 different attempts at creating the Dyson. I would also imagine that trying 5,000 times doesn't leave much time for complaining. His patience and persistence would lead him to make over a billion dollars with his invention.

But how do you have patience when you are ready to conquer the world today? More harm than good can come from trying to rush an outcome. I've learned through personal experience. When your patience is waning, it helps to remember it's never as bad as you think. Even if you get 100 no's, you only need one yes—so wait for it!

Chad Hymas, one of the top 10 motivational speakers in the country, said, "When things don't happen right away, just remember that it takes six months to build a Rolls Royce and 13 hours to build a Toyota."

After hitting rock bottom and turning my life around I wanted everything to be perfect right away. I wanted my wife to come home. I wanted her to forgive me as soon as I said I was sorry and I wanted to be back on top financially and professionally. Each one of those things happened but not without an incredible amount of patience on my part.

Being patient made me humble. I knew there were things that were outside of my control, like Jess forgiving me. But I also knew that she needed time to trust me again. I understood the concept of time and forgiveness but it didn't make it any easier. What made the wait bearable was knowing there was something great on the other side of that waiting. I have two beautiful daughters because I was blessed enough to get a second chance with Jess. The waiting I had to do is completely insignificant.

Now let's take a look at the second part of Step 6; being persistent.

My first experience with this came while I was still in college. Most college students are perpetually struggling for money. Tuition, books, housing— just simply every day living—is incredibly expensive. Finding enough extra cash for a pizza and soft drinks is an awesome day.

When Jess and I got married we started off living in an apartment. It was in the married housing section at school so we could save money. Our budget was practically non-existent, so I worked any job that I could find.

I quickly learned being a waiter was the way to go. Put a smile on your face, wow the customers, add a lot of hustle and the tips roll in. But it is one of the toughest jobs in the world. Many waiters dream of quitting on a daily basis! But this is where step 6 comes into play.

Working in a restaurant, for many, is their way of digging in so they can get to the next level in life. They are going to school, feeding their kids, or like Jess and I, saving for a home. Most importantly, the restaurant life teaches you the importance of serving others.

When you are a waiter, just showing up and looking pretty doesn't pay you enough to live. A waiter must "deliver" to get paid. And it is HARD! Learning this at a young age had a profound impact on my life.

During a particularly grueling day, a woman stopped me as I began to clear her table. She offered me a job at her company! Kathy Steward owned a local mortgage business. I had no idea she had been watching me hustle around the restaurant. She said she noticed my sense of urgency and pride in making sure my customer had the best dining experience. She explained my work ethic was exactly what she was looking for in an employee. I thought of all the times I wanted to throw in the towel. I dreamed of quitting so many times. But I stayed and worked as hard as I could. And doing that is what eventually led to my livelihood.

From my first days working for Kathy to my career today, I have worked step 6 many times. My profession has changed from the mortgage business, to the music industry, to an Inc. 5000 marketing, PR and software company. But the need to dig in is always there as a part of the journey.

Show me a successful person and I will show you someone who understands the importance of this step. Take actor Emily Blunt for example. Saying she had a tough time at school is a huge understatement. From age 7 to 11, she couldn't get a complete sentence out without stuttering. She was an object of daily ridicule. Her biggest dream was to hold a complete conversation. And yet, this shy, young girl from London, England, carried on.

By junior high one of her teachers noticed her unstoppable spirit. She encouraged Emily to try out for the school play. Yes, the girl who couldn't get out a complete sentence was going to speak in front of an audience.

The teacher suggested that she overcome her disability by trying different accents. She also suggested she try doing different character voices. And with lots of effort and practice, it actually worked. Emily was great in that school play. By the end of her teens, she stuttered no more.

This shy little girl who never gave up and always gave her all went on to achieve unbelievable things. Today, she is an award-winning actress, writer, director, and household name.

In an interview with W magazine, she said, "I was a smart kid, and had a lot to say, but I just couldn't say it. It would just haunt me. I never thought I'd be able to sit and talk to someone like I'm talking to you right now."

Digging in when you want to quit can bring unbelievable success and joy. That's why this step is included in this book. When you persevere, like Emily, nothing can stand in your way—no matter what your dreams are.

But that is just part of step 6. I know I have to continually grow and so do you. To be great at anything, we must remain always the student, focused on the WHY and willing to learn more. Educate yourself on your purpose!

My assistant still puts time on my calendar each month for me to read. I've learned something in every self-help or business book I've picked up. Like the mentors I mentioned earlier, many books have given me much needed direction and shown me the way to go. They are a vast well of knowledge that I can't do without.

And finally, you have to know where you stand to continue to try. You must acknowledge your weaknesses. You have to see what role you are playing in holding yourself back. When times get tough, I have learned to look at my part in each situation. I have to own up to it and make a plan on how to do things differently.

Even though it's uncomfortable, I have taken time to acknowledge my weaknesses. For me, I struggle with the details. Many times I have had great intentions for what I "mean" to do in business, but it's not enough. Action is everything! So I plan for my weakness! By admitting where I'm not strong or naturally gifted I can work on these areas. That has helped me be a better father, husband and businessman

I also have to be realistic about how much more I will have to work, pay, etc. to continue to master my WHY. I have to recommit to the process.

Nothing in life worth having comes easily. If you dig deep, continuing to persevere, you will experience success in the long run. Winston Churchill once gave a commencement speech at his alma mater. On Oct. 29, 1941, he visited Harrow School. Some of the most memorable words he spoke were, "Never give in, never give in, never, never, never, never-in nothing, great or small, large or petty - never give in except to convictions of honor and good sense. Never yield to force; never yield to the apparently overwhelming might of the enemy."

In mastering your WHY, the enemy is doubt and impatience. The enemy is tiny things that fill your schedule and push your passion aside. The enemy is a setback, a frustration, a roadblock an obstacle of some sort. Dig in. Push through! Don't give in! Master your WHY!

STEP 6

EXERCISE

Contemplate:

Review the exercises from the previous steps so they are fresh in your mind. Understand that, like the saying goes, "how you do anything is how you do everything." Dig in and give your journey all you've got. Consider previous obstacles you have faced. How did you overcome them? Consider what your biggest personal challenges may be for moving forward. And understand some parts of your journey will take awhile. Where do you struggle with patience? Knowing your challenges is half the battle.

Formulate:

What are your weaknesses? Take some time to consider them and write them down. Invest some time in developing possible actions that can counteract and improve these weaknesses. It's often when those weaknesses show up that we start to grow impatient.

Now is a time to add someone to your support team who will balance out your weaknesses with their strengths.

Activate: To help with being patient, stop. Take a break. Play golf, read a book, see a movie, take a trip or do whatever you need to do to refresh your mind. Hit the restart button. Patience is easier when you are engaged in life. Nothing comes from sitting around waiting and complaining. Acknowledge that good things come to those who wait. Allow the Universe time to put the right people in your life and open the doors you need to continue to master your WHY.

Accountability will help you be persistent. Seek out a mentor or team member who excels in the areas where your personal brilliance does not lie. Then you can maximize your efforts in your areas of strength. Put your plan to improve your weaknesses into action.

STEP 7
Accept or Adapt

"God, give us grace to accept with serenity the things that cannot be changed, Courage to change the things which should be changed, and the Wisdom to distinguish the one from the other."

— Reinhold Niebuhr

This is one of the greatest moments in your journey. You have reached a fork in the road and part of mastering your WHY is understanding this. You will certainly grow through this process and with growth comes change. By now you may have learned more about your purpose and might need to move in a different direction. You may be trying to force a square peg in a round hole. Or you may be exactly where you need to be and right on track. This is the point where we stop to figure that out.

Everybody's journey is different. And in pursuing your WHY the world opens up to you! By taking these steps you have hyper-focused your energy on a mission. And the more you learn the more you may realize the mission needs to change.

I thought I was destined to have a career in the mortgage business. And I was extremely successful at it. I built my career around a specific industry. I poured my heart and soul into creating a company that would be around for years. My WHY at the time was to help people buy homes. I wanted to help families live the American dream. I focused all my attention on growing and succeeding. But I never noticed my life was falling apart around me. This is where this step would have come in handy.

It's important to stop along the way and reflect on what is working and what needs to change. Your journey is like a river . You need to know the difference between moving towards your destination and trying to swim upstream. Where are you fighting the current and where have you come to a complete stand still? It's time to reflect on where you have been and where you want to go.

When I finally took the time to work this step I realized my WHY was still to help people but I was going about it the wrong way. It's why I took Potenza, a little company I started with my brother, and made it the catalyst for my WHY. I realized it didn't matter whether I was in the mortgage business or the marketing business. My WHY needed to be the center of everything I was doing.

Now I am continuing to work this step writing this book. The whole point of putting pen to paper is to share my journey with others so I can help them in some way. My story isn't perfect. I've had to share some pretty intimate things about my life and my journey. But with my WHY as my compass I am able to open up with ease. I accepted the fact the mortgage business was not the path I needed to continue on and I adapted my life and my career. I realized my company, Potenza, might not put me in the best environment to reach everyday people. I decided to adapt and write a book so others could learn from my story.

There is a great story of acceptance and adaptation that took place in my own hometown of Lafayette, LA. A long time ago young man came here to fly helicopters for the oil companies. When he was younger he struggled with his WHY. He couldn't decide between joining the military and pursuing a degree in literature. His family pushed him towards the military but his heart led him towards school. He graduated with a BA, summa cum laude, in literature. Then he received a Rhodes scholarship to Oxford University. While there he studied at Merton College. He graduated with a Master's Degree in English Literature. He knew his WHY and he was mastering it with passion.

But his family could not be discouraged and continued to push the military life. As many people often do he put his passion aside and started to pursue somebody else's WHY. He joined the U.S. Army and became a Captain. But even as he was climbing the ranks of the military his love of writing was always there.

After he finished his tour of duty with the Army he received an assignment to teach English Literature at West Point. This is where this step came in for him. He turned down the offer. His family disowned him for it but he had learned so much through his journey and he decided writing was his WHY. He accepted the rejection of his family. Then he adapted his dream from English Professor to songwriter. And somewhere in my own hometown he wrote the words to "Me and Bobby McGhee" and the rest is history. Kris Kristofferson must be a pro at this step. He walked the path towards his passion. He accepted the challenges and adaped his course when necessary no matter the cost.

It took me years to understand this process. I work on mastering it through the serenity prayer and meditation. In order for you to master it you must practice this step daily. Whether you include God at the beginning or not is up to you. I can't start my day without him. Each morning I meditate on the words, "God, grant me the serenity to accept the things I cannot change. The courage to change the things I can and the wisdom to know the difference." Every day starts with a clear understanding that some things are out of my control. I also acknowledge that with work I am able to adapt and make changes when necessary. The fact that I am human means I won't always know the difference between the two. Meditating helps me remember that and it keeps me grounded.

This ebb and flow of knowing when to accept and when to adapt are a big part of mastering your WHY. Mastering this step will help you go the distance and will enable you to have the endurance to finish. It's part of walking in the ART of your WHY. And it can't be a random practice every now and then. It's imperative to discipline yourself to look at this everyday.

I like how Nolan Ryan put it when he said, "Enjoying success requires the ability to adapt. Only by being open to change will you have a true opportunity to get the most from your talent."

Today I am slow to make big decisions. I always lean on the wisdom of people who have gone before me while taking some time to let this step play out. It has never failed me. And if you focus on mastering this step you too will know which path to take.

STEP 7
EXERCISE

Contemplate

Consider meditating each morning using the serenity prayer. Then ask yourself, "What isn't working? What am I trying to force?" And reflect on your journey so far. What have you learned that might need to be adjusted? Are you still headed in the same direction or should you change course? Meditation and ongoing contemplation will help you find the answers to these important questions.

Formulate

Determine the milestones on your journey that have not happened yet. If they are still an integral part of your WHY make a plan for making them happen. Perhaps you have changed course and find new milestones need to be added. Old ones may need to be removed. Make the change.

Make a list of the new milestones. Take the list you created and determine which ones you have control over and which ones you can't change. The ones you don't have control over may take longer. Or you may need to make some adjustments. Give your milestones a deadline.

Activate:

Each day choose one of your milestones. Work on adapting and making the changes needed to cross that milestone off your list! You can download a worksheet from our website at theartofwhy.com that will help you do this!

STEP 8
See Failures As Opportunities

"Winners are not afraid of losing.
But losers are. Failure is part of the process
of success. People who avoid failure also
avoid success."

— Robert T. Yiyosaki

There is something amazing going on in Livermore, California, at 4550 East Avenue. Documentary filmmakers from as far as France, Germany and England have traveled to this small town. The subject of their films is a historic item housed at fire station No. 6. This unique spectacle is in the Guinness Book of World Records and has been noted by Ripley's Believe it or Not.

But if it weren't for perseverance, it may never have existed at all.

The Centennial Light is the longest-lasting bulb in the world. It has been glowing for more than 110 years. When Thomas Edison set out to create a practical incandescent light he faced nothing but failure.

Through the roughest times, it was his attitude that helped him through. "I have not failed," he said.

"I've just tried 10,000 ways that didn't work."

If Edison would have quit when things got tough, we might all still be in the dark.

When I had my first real failure in business, I was crushed. I had shut down my mortgage business and during that time, it felt like my career was over. I wondered where I was going to go from there. Would I ever make that kind of money again? What would I do? Fears and insecurities began to seep into my brain.

Now, looking back, I see that what I had perceived as a failure was actually part of the process. It enabled me to find the next level of success. By persevering through the challenges I built my mental muscle. I was able to reach heights that before seemed insurmountable. My WHY kept me pressing on no matter what. You must always remember, your WHY is worth fighting for!

Let me share with you a little story about a woman who knew how to fight for her WHY.

Jill Blashack Strahan is the co-founder of her company, Tastefully Simple. It's multimillion-dollar business and one of the fastest growing companies in America.

Sitting outside staring at the business she started

in her backyard shed, Jill was about to call it a day and "get a real job." She was three months behind on her house payment. She wasn't even sure she could make the next payroll for her two employees. But then she took a deep breath and thought again. This was her dream. So she went back to work.

But as soon as her company began to take off, she was hit by a double tragedy. Her brother, Mike, was killed in a fire. And just a few months later, her husband suddenly died. She was left to raise her 5-year-old son on her own.

Jill admits she was bitter and angry. But she decided she wasn't going to let this tragedy stop her. Her husband and brother wouldn't want that. It was tempting to sulk in her pain, and she would have been justified doing so. But Jill determined that she was going to turn her pain into her passion to live out her dreams.

Through the rough times, Jill learned how amazing the human spirit could be. And when the going gets tough, action is always the choice to make. "Obstacles don't stop people," she says. "People stop themselves."

In my business, I have seen many doors close, and at times I was scared. I'll never forget when the first long term client decided to take his business elsewhere. Our relationship ultimately came to an end. I saw this as a gigantic failure! Little did I know at the time that this would turn out to be nothing more than a stumbling block. It was followed by the fastest growth my company had ever experienced—almost 500%!

Had we held on for dear life to this client, we would not have been able to grow the way we did. I might not have looked for innovative ways to strengthen and increase our business.

At some point on this journey you will encounter unwelcome interruptions. Learning to expect them can help you keep it together at the first sign of failure or disappointment.

Nick Woodman, the founder of GoPro, experienced failure before discovering his greatest opportunity. Before creating GoPro, Nick had two companies that crashed and burned. And I'm sure each experience left him devastated. But the two companies failing cleared the way for something greater.

The California native went off on a surfing odyssey to Australia and Indonesia. He wanted to clear his head after working on the other companies. While there, he noticed the film straps that tethered cameras to surfers easily broke. He wanted to make a better one. The idea for GoPro was born.

To start the company, Nick moved back in with his parents at 26 and worked eighteen- to twenty-hour days. To raise cash, he sold bead and shell belts out of the back of his VW van. He started GoPro with just $10,000.

And what a success! In 2004, GoPro ended the year with $150,000 in sales. In 2014, just 10 years later, GoPro's estimated worth was over $2.5 billion dollars. Was it easy? Absolutely not! But Nick kept moving forward despite his failures.

Throughout this rocky process, Nick found his WHY. In his own words: "GoPro helps people capture and share their lives' most meaningful experience with others—to celebrate them together. Like how a day on the mountain with friends is more meaningful than one spent alone, the sharing of our collective experiences makes our lives more fun."

As far as the tough times, Nick has a lot to say about that, too. "Seeing GoPro grow and become as successful as it is feels really good . . .. As an entrepreneur, it's a dark forest you're going through. And there's scary things in there and you just plow ahead," he said in an interview in 2011.

I have learned to plow through the challenges. I have come to trust that sometimes God allows these roadblocks. They force me to look in a certain area of my life that needs a course correction. I need a power greater than myself to lead me through difficult times. Having Him allows me to change with grace and see me through to the next level. In these moments, my faith is strengthened because God is there every time.

You must be open to these interruptions. You must see your failures as lessons that teach you how to do better the next time around. If you can master this you will never look at "faulire" the same way again.

STEP 8
EXERCISE

Contemplate:

Review the exercises from the previous steps so they are fresh in your mind. And then think about areas where you may have felt like you failed in the past. What lessons did you learn? What can you pull from that experience that will make you stronger moving forward?

Formulate

Make a page with 3 columns. In Column #1, put the specific Failure or Issue you are encountering. In Column 2, put your part in the issue. In Column #3, write possible solutions. Column 3 should not be done alone. Use your mentor and team to help you. No matter how small the issue is, try to be thorough.

Activate

Take the action items from Column 3 and decide which items can be worked on daily. For the non-daily items, make sure you set a completion date for each issue. On that date you test the progress and add more changes until the solution is complete. PLEASE NOTE: This process will be repeated 100s of times over the course of your journey. This is the road to true evolution!

STEP 9

Celebrate Your Milestones

"Celebrate what you've accomplished, but raise
the bar a little higher each time you succeed."

— Mia Hamm

Bart Connor is an Olympic gymnast. Less than a year before the 1984 Olympics, Bart tore his bicep muscle. For most athletes of his caliber, this type of injury would signal the end of a career. But not Bart. Just nine months later, he brought home two gold medals from Los Angeles.

So how did he overcome such odds? Bart told broadcaster Charlie Jones that he grew up celebrating his successes. "As a child, my parents would ask me every night before bed 'What was your success today?'" Bart said. "So I went to bed a success every night of my life. I woke up every morning a success. When I was injured before the Olympics, I knew I was going to make it back because I was a success every day of my life."

A celebration is a form of positive reinforcement. It actually teaches your subconscious mind to do more of what brought about the celebration. It likes the rewards and wants to repeat it. So celebration can lead to more positive thinking and more success. Celebrating life is a mental and emotional choice. If you don't stop to celebrate your success you run the risk of getting lost in the pursuit of it.

To use gratitude in your life, you need more than just an awareness of its existence. You need to adopt the attitude of celebrating life in everything you do. I invite you to do what Bart Conner's parents did with him as a child. Ask yourself every night before you go to bed, "What was my success for today?" Celebrate that success before you close your eyes at night and again when you awaken the next morning.

Step 9 is about celebrating when milestones are achieved. It's about expressing gratitude for their occurrence in your life.

At my company, Potenza, the last few years have been prosperous. But getting here has been incredibly tough, with a lot of extra work for my whole team. So last year, I started looking for creative ways for our team to come together outside of the office. I wanted to celebrate their accomplishments and show them my appreciation for their efforts.

I began taking my entire staff on retreats we call "vision days." In the past, I would have thought this was a waste of valuable money-making time.

But I came to realize the importance of celebration and appreciation in the workplace. Celebrating brings my staff closer together and let's them know their hard work is paying off.

On these vision days, we discuss where the company is going and how we're going to get there. We laugh together, eat together, and talk about good times and war stories from this year and years past. We simply spend time together celebrating how far we've come and where we are today!

What happens when we take the time to celebrate? We come back excited and refreshed with a renewed passion about WHY we do what we do. Success becomes part of our culture, and we start to look for and expect more of it!

I first started focusing on this step after talking with my friend Olivia. I've known her for many years, and she's one of the most talented, confident writers I've ever met. She has an incredibly successful freelance career, with national magazines clamoring for her work.

But Olivia's career didn't start out that way. In fact, in the beginning, every time she sat down to write, she was full of fear and self-doubt. She had no formal training as a journalist. She actually started her career as a file clerk at a small-town weekly newspaper.

Olivia occasionally wrote some of her own stories. One day, her editor announced they were submitting a few of them to a state writing contest. Olivia won. She beat entries from journalists all across the state. The publishing company sent her and her editor to the state capitol to claim her prize. The owners of that small town newspaper understood the importance of celebrating milestones. When she returned the entire newspaper staff honored her win with a huge party.

Olivia went on to overcome her fears and self doubts. She became the highly sought after writer she remains today. She credits those early celebrations as the catalyst for her success.

My company received its biggest honor to date. We have made the Inc. 5000 list; a ranking of the TOP 5,000 fasting growing private companies in America according to Inc. Magazine. As the son of missionaries who nearly lost it all, it was a defining moment for me.

Jess and I flew to Phoenix to attend the Inc. 5000 award ceremony. I'll never forget standing in that auditorium with the person I love most being told, "You are doing an incredible job." That feeling of validation and celebration had me flying high.

As a society we have gotten so good at doing the exact opposite of celebrating the milestones. We're often trained to downplay our success than to blow our own horn.

But here's the clincher. If you focus on self-deprecation, you'll get more of the stuff you don't want to celebrate. If you focused on celebrating your milestones that leads to more success and celebration. You get what you focus on. You need to celebrate your milestones! It's crucial to keeping your WHY alive and thriving.

Celebrating your milestones will also build faith in yourself and those around you. It's about looking back and seeing what you and God have accomplished together and the blessings that He has sent your way. And most importantly, it's about-facing the future full of gratitude and celebration!

STEP 9
EXERCISE

Contemplate

What Successes [even small ones] have come about from pursuing your WHY? What goals can you celebrate completing?

Formulate

Write a list of the "Monuments" [achieved goals from working the steps 1-8] you need to celebrate. Make a list of the people in your life that you believe deserve a monument. Write out the way you feel will best celebrate them. You also need to keep a list each day of anything that **you** accomplished.

Activate

Set up a time or event to celebrate your goals. Build a monument or trophy or plaque/frame on behalf of your successes. Make a Gratitude List to stay positive. Write out a list each day of all the things you are grateful for. This will help you recognize the wins happening in your journey. This will also help you through the stumbling blocks along the way. It's important to stay hopeful and enjoy the ride. Staying consistent with a gratitude list will make sure you are celebrating your milestones, no matter how big or small.

STEP 10

Start Over and Give Back

"The true meaning of life is to plant trees under whose shade you do not expect to sit."

— **Nelson Mandela**

Each time I take this journey I find I am a different man on the other side. And although the specifics of my WHY have changed over time I am always drawn to this final step. My WHY is to help others; to take my failures, my stumbling blocks, my triumphs and my success and share it with others.

To achieve greatness you must pass along your knowledge. To truly perfect the art of YOUR WHY you have to give back. It's really that simple.

The path you have been on has been long and arduous. You have had many ups and downs but you have reached one of the most important points in your journey. Everything you've been through and all the hard work you've put in is rich with experience. You have successfully walked a path that others are still lost on. Although it may feel like an end, it is really just the beginning. And I am excited to help you get started!

But before we jump in let's take a moment to reflect on your journey.

To discover your purpose, you had to understand your WHY. To start the journey, you had to take a hard look at the costs or the investment of time. Next you made a conscious and dedicated decision to start honing your craft.

You built a team around you of people who would support you and lift you up. You forged relationships to build a family of others who helped you perfect your WHY.

Then, the real work began! You started taking one step at a time on a path to living the life you were born to live. You started focusing on your purpose daily.

But there have been times when you thought it was too tough. You wanted to quit or just settle in and let whatever happens, happen.

You didn't give in. You continued to work! And it was during the times when life distracted you or the world seemed to put a roadblock at every turn that you really started to shine.

And the hard work and dedication started to pay off! You caught glimpses of the sun through the clouds. This journey is an up-and-down road with huge inclines and difficult times throughout the process. But you've learned that good things come to those who wait.

And in the end, you celebrated! You've been able to look back at all you have accomplished and learned. If you have worked the steps, you are most likely a different person from the one who started this journey. And you've seen changes in your life as a direct result of your efforts. And you now understand that your WHY is truly an art form!

You can now give yourself a pat on the back and say, " I did it. I've finished the journey!"

But wait. Perhaps now is a good time for me to tell you the journey has just begun.

You see you can't really hone your craft without this final step.

The art of WHY is about living your purpose and becoming the best version of who you are. But the reason for doing that is so you can give the best you have to the world around you.

You had to get to Step 10 before you could really begin!

The greatest success in this world is incredibly hard to measure and quantify. You can't measure it with money or material possessions. If those were the true measures, then Ghandi and Mother Teresa would be epic failures.

Don't get me wrong. You don't have to dedicate your life to poverty to succeed. Money, for many, is a byproduct of success. But it is definitely not the way to gauge the value of the life you are living.

The greatest success comes from the sum total of the relationships you develop with a higher power and those around you, while living your WHY. And the more you give to these relationships, the more successful you will be!

The first time I worked the 10 Steps, I did it to heal and to grow. Every time since then I have continued to heal and grow. But now I do it while serving those around me and helping them to master their WHY!

Each time you work the steps, you'll grow and the world around you will benefit. It's mind-boggling if you reflect on the simplicity of this truth. By investing yourself in others, you gain more than you could ever give away.

Let's look at this from another perspective.

There is an energy that flows through all of us. The Hindus call it prana. It's known as qi or chi in

China. It is mentioned in over 95 other cultures as well. This energy is said to constitute the source of life that is so often associated with soul, spirit, and mind.

As Humans, it's natural for us to take the energy that flows through us and try to keep it or hold on to it. I believe that all human are wired like capacitors. Capacitors have one job: slow the energy down. Without them our household appliances would be fried from the 110-220 volts passing through them. They serve an important role. I believe humans by nature take on energy the same way.

Imagine an electronic board filled with capacitors slowing the energy down. Now imagine that the board is the earth and we as humans are the capacitors. If one of the capacitors is removed from the board than that part of the board is able to let energy flow uninhibited. That uninhibited energy is now available to be redistributed to more capacitors.

I believe this energy is agnostic and wants to flow freely. So one day I asked myself, what would happen if I removed myself from the role of the capacitor and let the energy flow uninhibited through me?

I have been putting this theory to the test for the

past few years in my own life. My experiment is simple, make my life more about helping other people (in each aspect of my life) and see if the results in my life are different. The affects of this exercise have been staggering.

The energy I give out when I help others allows more energy to flow through me. The only way to let the energy flow through you is to give it away. You do this through service, generosity, selflessness and love. When applying these universal principles to life and business, the outcome is amazing.

This is the secret of greatness. You don't really own anything until you give it away! Think of it as philanthropy of the soul!

Now you have developed your WHY and you are starting a second journey through the steps. It's time to give back! Your WHY needs to be for the greater good of the whole.

I used to think life was like a ladder. You spend your days trying to work your way to the top. I was pretty disappointed when I found out I was wrong.

It wasn't until I accepted the idea that you don't ever get to the top of the ladder that I really got it. You have to understand this journey is not a ladder but a circle.

We often compare our lives to those who are in front of us—the people who have more or who have accomplished more. But it's those behind us who haven't come as far that need the attention.

If we could all look back and help those who haven't walked the path yet, there would always be room for someone to move ahead. You have to give back to keep moving forward. Step 10 is about coming full circle and doing it in every aspect of your life.

Before the age of 25, I had gone on more than 25 mission trips. I always felt fulfilled when I came home. Things felt right with the world. But that feeling passed over time. I didn't practice Step 10 on a daily basis, so I had no way to keep that joy.

It wasn't until I got sober that I uncovered a way to practice this principle of giving my time and myself to other people on a daily basis. By sponsoring others who are in recovery, I have a firm grasp on the idea of being a servant leader.

The number-one way to give back is to invest time into other people's lives with no expectation of any return on that investment.

There was a time in my life when I wondered what in the world people meant when they said, "Time is more valuable than money."

I thought it was absurd because, as I said earlier, I wanted to be wealthier, more powerful, and more important. I thought money was the most powerful thing! But time is the MOST valuable thing. You can't create it, you can't get it back and you have no idea how much you'll have until it runs out!

You need to be intentional about your relationships and make giving a part of your lifestyle. If you don't master Step 10, you won't ever master the art of your WHY!

Through this step, I realized there are opportunities for giving throughout my day. I didn't need to travel to a third world country to give back. I didn't need to go on a mission trip or work in an orphanage to make a difference. Step 10 has become a way of life. I am constantly looking for opportunities to practice this part of the art of WHY.

I didn't understand the full value relationships have until I had my first child. It was my first undeniable glimpse of the great reward of giving instead of taking.

Children have no concept of money; their only currency is time. And not just time, but quality time. So for a father like me, who is a preoccupied, workaholic by nature, this type of giving does not come easy.

Today, my children are a huge priority. Over the past five years, I have made a point to be present for my children. Though they are still young, I can already feel the positive impact it has when I am present in my time with them.

I can miss 100 client meetings. But I can't miss my daughter's piano recital. The truth is that writing a check would be easier at times than giving your time. But time is one of the greatest sacrifices a person can make and such a true and valuable gift to give.

Some of the greatest leaders, writers, and visionaries have spoken about the importance of living a life of purpose. Here are a few of my favorite quotes from people who were passionate about mastering their WHY.

"What counts in life is not the mere fact that we have lived. It is what difference we have made to the lives of others that will determine the significance of the life we lead."

— Nelson Mandela

"I've learned that you shouldn't go through life with a catchers mitt on both hands. You need to be able to throw something back."

— Maya Angelou

"How wonderful that no one need wait a single moment to improve the world."

— Anne Frank

"Anyone who thinks that they are too small to make a difference has never tried to fall asleep with a mosquito in the room."

— Christine Todd Whitman

"Only a life lived for others is a life worthwhile."

— Albert Einstein

"From what we get, we can make a living; what we give, however, makes a life."

— Arthur Ashe

STEP 10
EXERCISE

Contemplate

What would you add to your WHY after getting farther into your journey? As you prepare to start over how can you make your WHY even more about helping other people get what they need? Who will you help?

Formulate:

Take a look at your contract you signed in the beginning. Make sure to add new challenges and new goals for yourself as you prepare to begin again. Add some new aspects that make it even more "others" focused. This will make the WHY more about giving back. Add something to your contract that makes you less of a capacitor!

Activate

Now it's time to start over and bring someone with you. Make sure you choose someone who is receptive to the idea of mastering his or her WHY. Mentoring is one of the best ways to share your experience with someone and to help him or her master their own WHY. Having worked through the steps already you will be wiser and more experienced. You will be a part of the team they will build. You will help them learn to be patient, to know when to accept or adapt and when to dig in. Your experience will be different each time and you will learn new things on every journey.

FINAL STEP

Give a copy of the Art of Why to someone else. You can also register a copy at **bookcrossing.com** and see where the world takes it! You never know how the universe will respond to you once you become a capacitor for giving back.

If you give back hoping to gain something, often you will get nothing. It was Ghandi who said, "The best way to find yourself is to lose yourself in the service of others."

And once you have lost yourself in the spirit of giving back, start over at Step 1!